THE LITTLE BOOK

FROM THIS TO BLISS

LARRY DANIEL WEBB

Edited by
Robert Allen Geida

MERAKI PUBLISHING COMPANY
CONNECTICUT, USA

Copyright © 2020 by Larry Daniel Webb

All rights reserved. This book or any portion thereof may
not be reproduced or used in any manner whatsoever
without the express written permission of the author.

This book is not intended to be a substitute for the medical
advice of a licensed physician. The reader should consult
with their doctor in any matters relating to his/her health.

Printed in the United States of America
First Printing March 2020

ISBN: 978-1-7322974-2-5

MERAKI PUBLISHING COMPANY
Connecticut, USA
www.merakipublishingcompany.com
Carolyn Geida, graphic designer
Robert Geida, editor
Pamela DiMaio, proofreader
Photographs: Bigstock.com

Contents

Foreword
v

Preface
vii

The Group
1

Recovery to Rediscovery
9

Faith versus Fear
23

Pilots and Bikers
39

Illusion
47

Pharmaceuticals
51

Meditation
57

Epilogue
63

About the Author
65

Foreword

"From Recovery to a Rediscovery of Life's Bliss"

My name is George Hayes and have been blessed with the opportunity to write my thoughts about *The Little Book*. I appreciate Larry Daniel Webb with trusting me to share my thoughts.

I am the following: Licensed Clinical Social Worker, Licensed Alcohol and Drug Counselor, and recovering addict with over 35 years Clean.

I am trained in the medical model, 12 step programs, medication management and rational recovery.

That being said, I chose to read the book with a bit of skepticism, but that was quickly challenged as I learned about Bliss and his approach to rediscovery.

Mr. Webb's ability to offer a uniquely different look to all aspects of rediscovery and challenge the essence of recovery.

"The Little Book" author Larry Daniel Webb takes the reader on an informative journey about alternatives to traditional treatments.

As a recovering person, FEAR has always been defined as Face Everything And Recover. These words are challenged in the book and mean: False Evidence Appearing Real.

What emerges from that is a healthy new outlook for all whom choose to read this book. Covering everything from medication, addiction, support groups, and faith, to finding purpose an everchanging world.

George Hayes Jr., LCSW, LADC

> I was once asked how long does it take for someone to recover from an addiction. The answer in truth is in an instant.

Preface

*"It's 2020, and we as
a people still can't see."*

This is a statement I wrote in 1967 and somehow it still holds true today. In this world of such great technology and vast information we tend to miss or distort the simplest of truths that have been around since the beginning of time. What we don't see are simplistic truths that create our reality. What we must see is that everything that becomes reality must first begin with a thought and from that thought manifestation of our reality emerges. We still follow old beliefs even though time has transcended them, very much as if we choose to use candlelight as our main source for bringing light to darkness even though electricity exists. What gets distorted and missed is that we create our own reality. This book is written to shed light on the darkness of the world of addiction and to simplify our methods for manifesting our desired reality. The title "The Little Book," is not a statement or a knock on any step-by-step program or on any other available treatment. The title is intended to draw the attention to those who struggle with addiction and to shed light on the simple truths that can bring each person on this journey, from recovery to a rediscovery of life's bliss.

The light that I wish to shed on the world of addiction is the light of energy vibration. This is a light that we all possess and in essence is who we are at the core of our being. Once this rediscovering becomes clear in our consciousness and we manifest it into our lives, we transcend to living our lives in recovery and walk the journey in a feeling of bliss.

I was once asked how long does it take for someone to recover from an addiction. The answer in truth is in an instant. In an instant you say? I know that many will struggle with the idea that someone could recover from an addiction in an instant. This statement, as well as many other statements that this book will offer, will be discomforting and leave many readers uneasy. Many experts and professionals will adamantly disagree with this statement and back it up with statistics and studies in this field. I will be the first to say that I am not a doctor or a scientist and possess no degrees claiming to be. I also can't dispute any statistics or studies. I am simply suggesting a train of thought vibration that has the potential to change your life as you know it from here forward. Even though you may read something that does not sit well with you, I urge you to stay open and relinquish your need to judge. As you read you might find that much will resonate with your higher self, for it already knows truth. When I speak of your higher self, spirit, or God I'm not speaking in religious terms. I am speaking about our oneness with the divine universal energy that flows through all of us regardless of what you choose to call it. This book is written in simple language because in truth, healing addiction can be simple. It has been said that simplicity can be very hard for the confused mind to understand. I say to you keep this simple and remember that easy does it. May you go from this to bliss.

Namaste,

Larry Webb

THE GROUP

Introductions

Good morning, Namaste; my name is Chit Bliss; most people who know me just call me Bliss to keep it simple because people always pronounce my first name wrong. Feel free to just call me Bliss. I am going to be here for the next four hours to guide anyone interested in healing an addiction. In all honesty, four hours is actually overkill to accomplish this simple goal, but we will use and honor the time allotted. During this time I will speak briefly about a couple of concepts that you will need to adopt to make dramatic changes. Most of the time, I will field any questions that you might have. The last half-hour we will practice meditation which will tie everything neatly together.

Some of you will find it difficult to accomplish this goal in such a short time. Remember: it's only as hard as you make it. This will be a journey that will shake up your reality like never before; I promise you that. I am honored to be here and excited to share this experience with you. None of what I share with you will be new to you really, because actually it's all about remembering. Many of you look puzzled by that statement, but in truth we are all born with this knowing of truth. Therefore, it is remembering that we shall return to our consciousness. Why don't we go around the circle and have you briefly introduce yourselves and I will do my best to remember your names. After that I will answer any questions that you might have about this group. Let's just say before we begin so we can get past the obvious; drugs work. They do what they are designed to do. Addiction and drugs are intertwined, yet they are the same. Okay that idea is done and out of the way. All right then let's start with you, my brother.

The Group

My name is Terry, I'm an addict, and I am in recovery. My drug of choice is heroin, and I have been clean for 8 days.

Hi, I'm Gary and my drugs of choice are marijuana and alcohol.

Steve, I am an addict, my drug of choice is cocaine; I have been in recovery for 2 months and 5 days. This is my 4th time in this program so this time I hope to get it right.

My name is Ericka and I am addicted to sex and coke. I had dirty urine yesterday so I probably won't be here tomorrow. (Scattered laughter fills the room).

Cindy, I love to drink. I am court ordered to be here, which is better than being in jail. I guess Oxytocin is the drug that got me here.

I'm Walter, and I use crack and I am sick and tired of being sick and tired, so if you have a miracle bring it dude.

Lisa, I just smoke pot and drink, and I'm court mandated with possession and intent to sell.

My name is Trish and I am addicted to pain pills.

I am Lamar and I love gambling and drinking, which always seems to get me into trouble.

Sheila, just got out of detox yesterday, crystal meth is my lover.

Tony, I love the high from heroin but it doesn't love me.

Question: Bliss you're from the hood way back, right?
BLISS: Yes, right! Back then everybody called me Chet. Seems like a lifetime ago.

I remember back in the day when you used to get torn up.
BLISS: Right again. I chased that dragon through the darkness for many years.

So what happened to you and how did you wind up here? Are you going to share your story? Most counselors won't even admit that they have had a drug problem. Some kind of rule? Steve chimed in anxiously.
BLISS: I am not really that type of counselor. To be real straight with you, I have no degrees at all. Let's just say that I'm not only a guy named Bliss, but someone who knows how to live in bliss with immense gratitude for every day. Essentially I am here to offer you an alternative to traditional treatment. Which is to say that I'm not interested in doing behavior modification. Although that may be the standard practice in many treatment facilities, you'll find that in the long run it will fail. Of course it would be pleasing to anyone around you to see your disturbing behavior stop. But if we don't get to the core of your beliefs, we have simply put a Band-Aid on the problem that is causing the behavior. First, I will tell my story and then you can ask your questions. Fair enough? (The group nods in agreement.) So here's the story of what happened to me; I was a mess, totally lost in the dark world of drugs then one day I simply walked down a different path — Okay, questions?

That's your story? You walked a different path?
BLISS: That's it, sorry I can't make it more elaborate.

THE GROUP

You mean to tell us that you just walked away from your addiction by just changing directions?

BLISS: Yes, even more powerful I changed my mind. You should all rejoice you all have that choice. The power of choice is the power of change. So yes I chose to take a different direction. You know in Zen it is said once you're facing the right direction, just keep walking.

You didn't go into a program?

BLISS: No I simply changed my program, pretty much like changing the channel on your TV or radio; I tuned into a different frequency. I've heard it best described as if you're listening to a radio station on 950 AM but then you pick up on the frequency of 101 FM.

You don't go to meetings, or take medication? Because frankly this routine wears me out.

BLISS: Yes, I meet with myself every day and I use meditation instead of medication, which is what I will share with you today. Medication is great and has many benefits, but meditation is also great and has enormous benefits. You should embrace both into your experience. In some cases medication falls in line with behavior modification and becomes a Band-Aid to your experience. Your human body is an awesome pharmacy of its own and meditation is where you get your script. You have the ability to make your own medicine.

Our body makes medicine?

BLISS: Yes, in the right dose without all of the side affects. I promise we'll go deeper into that today.

I remember you used serious drugs like heroin and crack?

BLISS: I tasted that Dragon in many of its most immeasurable forms.

So now you just live in happiness? Sounds like bullshit to me. Terry said with a tone of disgust.

BLISS: Actually, I live in a state of bliss, which is a state of spiritual joy, pretty much happiness without all of the effort to be happy. Look, you don't have to believe any of this or even practice any of the tools that I share with you. In truth it's not my concern if you do or don't; I am just putting it out there for you to consider. Some of you may take this on your journey and others may not. I speak to you from the heart; if you like your current circumstances on the path that you're on, please, by all means, do what works for you. I don't say this with any sarcasm; some will be ready to receive this information and others will not. I don't make any determinations or judgments on where any of you are on your journey in this life. It's easy to see where you are in this moment, so while I have this time with you I will shed some light on the darkness that is addiction. Each one of you will determine where you go from here. Once again, I am not asking you to believe everything that you hear; I am simply asking you to listen and determine what resonates with you.

So if I like smoking pot and drinking, you're saying that I should continue?

BLISS: I'm saying that if this is what pleases you and resonates with your soul, by all means follow your bliss. If the road you're on that led you to this room and many programs like it and it's in alignment with your happiness, then you're in the right place. On the other hand, if this has not been your cup of tea, I will show you a different path and its up to you to decide which way to proceed. Quite frankly it's all as simple as that. In truth your true soul knows your real calling and it will continue to call to you. Everything that I will share with you today your soul already knows, you've just forgotten it.

I've been in and out of programs for the last 9 years of my life. How can this be as simple as that?

BLISS: The first thing that you must understand is that simplicity is very hard for the confused mind to understand. That is not a knock on anyone's mind; its just truth. So what we need to do is remove the confusion. Albert Einstein, one of the greatest minds of our time, once said; "You cannot solve a problem with the same min." Take a moment to ponder that. A lot of what we will talk about, some will find discomforting and uneasy because of beliefs you hold to be true. Other things will resonate with you because somewhere in your consciousness you believe it to be true. So all I will ask of you is to stay open minded and relinquish the need to judge. Remain open and let what you hear flow through your consciousness and allow your higher self to determine what is truth for you. This way if truth comes to you and knocks on your door you might let it in. I ask nothing more from you, for it is your higher self that already knows truth and it's your higher self that I am addressing. To make any major change in your life there are 2 factors that must be in place. Number 1, you must want it. Number 2, you must allow it. So assuming that you already want it, we now must concentrate on allowing it.

So how long have you been in recovery?

BLISS: I've been recovered for many years, double digits for sure, but I don't keep track, never have. I often get asked that question when I do these meetings of thought. Even more alarming is how many people I speak to that keep track of how long it's been. Somewhere we were taught to think that if we keep track of how long we have been so called clean, or remember where we have been, that it somehow enhances recovery. In truth, which is what this is all about, you are keeping active the event that you don't want in your thoughts. It's funny to me because at one time in each of our lives we've all had a bedwetting problem. Anyone here remember how long it's been since you last wet the bed? We can learn so much from children because they know how to let go of the past or unwanted behavior and move on. When a child is learning to walk, we don't watch them fall and say, "Oh, forget it; you could fall again." The older we get the more warnings we adapt to our daily lives. You see there is a big difference between being in recovery and being recovered. This is a great place to begin. Let me go further into this question.

> **The Power of Choice is the Power of Change.**

Recovery to Rediscovery

"Everything is energy." Another great quote from Albert Einstein. This is important as we move along, because not only have many indigenous cultures practiced energy healing, but also today modern science is concurring with this truth. Quantum physics supports the fact that one of the most powerful forms of energy is thought. Thoughts become things. So as we change our thoughts, we change things. Thoughts are powerful, but words are even more powerful. From these two powers we get the greater power of action. We must be aware that our actions manifest our thoughts. Now here is the key— your feelings or emotions are the ultimate power in manifesting things into our reality. As powerful as your mind is, the feelings and emotions from your heart or inner being is what will unfold as your experience. Your heart is the most powerful energy center of your body, not the brain. If you question the idea that your heart isn't more powerful than your brain, you only need to think of how devastating you feel with a broken heart, or the overwhelming feeling that drives your soul when you fall in love. We must make the distinction between our thoughts and our feelings. I'm really speaking here about the distinction between recovery and rediscovery. This is a journey that we must all take.

What do you mean by the journey we must take?

BLISS: The journey from recovery or having and holding a thought or belief to a rediscovery, or the beginning of changing our thoughts and beliefs which generates words that lead to our actions or saying this another way: The meaning we give to the words we use becomes the meaning. For instance, let's take a statement used repeatedly in recovery as an example; "Once an addict always an addict." So the thought runs like this, "I am an addict." Right from the start we tell ourselves that we are addicts, something nobody would ever strive to be. Ask yourself, was it ever a goal of yours to become an addict?

Of course not, Bliss, but don't you first have to admit you are an addict?

BLISS: Let me repeat this and be very clear; words reinforce our thoughts and have great power. When we began today, I asked everyone to introduce themselves. Each one of you followed your name with your drug of choice. I simply asked for your name, yet all of you responded with a negative association to describe yourself. A couple of you even went so far as to call yourselves addicts.

Well that's who we are. Why should we lie to ourselves?

BLISS: You are what you say you are. What you hold your thoughts on and speak about with emotional feelings you will manifest into your life experience. Therefore the thought "I am an addict" is an illusion created by our mind; then it is compounded by your words and reinforced through other people's beliefs. Your beliefs are thoughts that you hold to be true for a long time. So what if those beliefs you hold are wrong?

The rediscovery is that we are the true creators of our experiences. So when asked to introduce myself, my reply was, "I am Chit Bliss." In my heart as I said that I truly felt a passion for life that I share with everyone I meet. I feel gratitude and honor for all that I have become. Now I've introduced a new thought followed by strong feelings in my soul and all the words that I use to create the action for new experiences.

I'm not sure I follow you, Bliss?

BLISS: What makes you feel better? When you say "I am an addict" what emotions are tied to that word addict? Where in the definition of the word is there a good feeling? Really get this; it's important to be aware of how you feel! Everything is birthed through those emotions.

The way you say it sounds easy, but it's not. How can you make such a simple claim about addiction when it's such a daily struggle for so many?

BLISS: Yes, I know, you make it sound so difficult when it's so simple for so many. The simple truth is that all of your power lies in the present moment. Your struggle is your belief that your past and your current circumstances are you now. In truth, your current circumstances is your past. Relinquish your need to defend what I said, just allow it to sit with you for one minute without judgment.

Sometimes if we look to nature, we get a clear picture of this journey from recovery to the rediscovery. Let us take a simple scenario of a child that finds a wounded bird with a broken wing in the backyard. The child brings the wounded bird to his mother who shares her child's empathy and does whatever she can to help nurture the wounded bird. She tapes the wing and nourishes the bird so that it may reach its optimum health. As time passes, the bird regains strength through this process and eventually the broken wing mends to the point where the tape is removed and the bird regains its use of the wing. At first the bird hops short distances and then increases to short flights. One day, the bird flies from the branch across the sky and off into the distance. As the mother and child observe the bird's flight across the sky neither one says, "Look that bird is in recovery." Even more important, the bird has relinquished its fear that its once damaged wing will fail again. The bird easily soars across the sky because that's what birds do.

Dr. Wayne Dyer gives another example of this metaphor when he shared his experience of being on an African safari some years back. Dr. Dyer recalls waking up one morning and seeing a herd of zebra grazing in a field. He goes on to describe how one particular zebra had its hind leg torn and shredded so that the blood and flesh were vividly exposed. Intrigued, Dr. Dyer asked one of the guards what had happened to that zebra. The guard replied that the previous afternoon a lion had gotten hold of the zebra, nearly taking its life. Fortunately the zebra managed to escape this traumatic event. As Wayne gazed back at the zebra, he had the most insightful thought, "and it's grazing here this morning." So the question we must ask ourselves is why is it that the supposed less intelligent creature adapts and moves on so quickly and we humans remain so long in the state of recovery. The difference is the mindset to move on.

Wait a minute Bliss, you're referring to injuries in animals not a disease in humans. I mean isn't an addiction a disease?

BLISS: The answer is no in the true sense of the word. If you take the origin of the word it means Dis-ease, which would be correct when it comes to addiction because you are in the state of dis-ease. Unfortunately the misuse of this word runs rampant and is a distortion of the true meaning. Today's society interprets the word disease to mean that you have a sickness that may or may not be treatable or curable. This distortion leads to disempowerment and a hopeless state of being. When someone finds him or herself in this situation, they normally yield all of their power to the person giving the diagnosis. Don't get me wrong. The person giving the diagnoses is a good and caring person, giving you the best of their knowledge from all that they have learned.

Yes, of course, they are doctors who have studied for years. I think they would know more than me and even you right?

BLISS: Yes, certainly in their area of study, but not in the areas they haven't studied. You see we must broaden your perception of what you know to be true.

You mean I am supposed to know more than my doctor?

BLISS: Depending on the subject matter, sometimes yes. Actually no one knows you better than you know yourself. In many cases even your doctor has to ask you questions about yourself before they can even begin a diagnosis. Before medication or treatment can be prescribed, there has to first be a diagnosis of a disease or disorder. Once the label of disease or disorder is applied, medication is dispensed as a part of a treatment. Doctors are highly skilled and highly educated individuals, without any doubt. Still, the fact remains and any doctor will tell you that your role in the healing process is strongly connected to your attitude and belief in the doctor. That speaks the loudest towards healing. We will go into this a little deeper later.

What did you mean by broadening our perception?

BLISS: I'm glad you asked, because that is the crux of this conversation. Hear this well, our reality is based on our perceptions. How you perceive things is how they are; no exception. This is the basis of your reality. Let's take a closer look at this perception broadening or changing right now. I'm talking about making a new shift of paradigm in your thoughts. You have beliefs which are just thoughts that you hold to be true. Suppose if what you believe is wrong? Let's look at a belief and see if we can make a shift right now. (The group gives an overall nod of agreement.) Okay, is it fair to say that you all believe that there are people who have multiple personalities? Good, so if I were to add that a person who has multiple personalities and is a diabetic can change personalities and in an instant that they go from Steve the diabetic to Sue, a person who believes that Sue has no trace of diabetes in the new personality? Some of you are having a change in perception, which is now a change in your reality.

RAMON: No way, of course not, he's still Steve.

BLISS: Actually, that is possible, it's true and not just with diabetes.

No way man. How could that be possible?

BLISS: It sounds so unbelievable coming from me, yet in the medical community this isn't astonishing at all; it's just common knowledge. In one case a lady was drinking at a party and people began to worry that she was drinking too much. So she simply responded "I will not drive home, one of my other personalities will." So she could actually switch personalities and become non-intoxicated in the conscious knowing that someone else was going to drive home sober. If a doctor or scientist told you the same thing, that not only with diabetes, but also with your vision that lesions could disappear and other physical qualities could change, you would have a Paradigm shift. Something that you hold to be true as your belief, now based on scientific proof changes when you have a paradigm shift, or change in belief.

So they can change personalities and change their physiology? So this person drinking alcohol would still have alcohol in their body and if they switched back later they would be intoxicated again?

BLISS: Exactly and when Sue would return to Steve, he once again would have diabetes. We need to get into the knowing.

That just seems so hard to believe. Can you clarify what this really means because I'm struggling with the whole idea?

BLISS: Yes, the wow is really that the only difference between you and this person with multiple personality disorder, scientifically, is that when Steve changes into Sue, he has no doubt that he is now Sue. The paradigm shift that we just experienced is that you held a belief to be true until you were awakened to a new belief or knowing. Some of you have not made the shift because you will need a doctor to quantify this as true. Amazingly enough most doctors understand this and are nonchalant when explaining it because it's just known. Now to further enhance your paradigm shift let's take the statement "once an addict, always an addict." This is a powerful statement that becomes a belief that you hold to be true. So, the question we must ask is; is it true? Scientifically the body changes over completely every 7 years. That is to say that you aren't even the same person physically, every cell in your body that was there seven years ago is gone and you have created a new body. So the person that you'd called an addict seven years ago has completely changed scientifically. Now if your thinking has not changed, you create all new cells with the same belief that you are an addict. So now let's change the statement. At one time I had an addiction and now I feel that I've left it behind and have moved on with my life. Who will I be in seven years?

So our bodies change according to our thoughts?
BLISS: On a cellular level yes, which then becomes your experiences. Without making this a science class, remember that cells have memory. The outside of every cell has a thin almost invisible circumference called a membrane. This membrane is the brain of the cell. Our bodies are not only made up of cells, but also are cells in action. The overriding determiner of our experiences begins with thought. "As you think, so shall you be" is not some hocus-pocus illusion. Today quantum physics and modern science are meeting at the same understanding. A lot of indigenous people have known this and have lived it for quite some time. Science has recently had its own shift changing so much of what we know to be true today. We all took science at some point and were taught that the nucleus of a cell was the brain at the center of the cell. It's now known that you can take the nucleus out of the cell and it will perform all functions without the nucleus. The meaning of that is catastrophic and is changing beliefs we once held as true.

Are you talking about yogi, sage and shaman when you say indigenous people?

BLISS: Yes to name a few.

So this multiple personality knows that he has changed into another personality without any doubt; I understand that. Now you're saying that our body changes over every seven years according to our thoughts and beliefs?

BLISS: Yes, thoughts held long enough become beliefs. It is the knowing that makes all the difference. You see when a knowing confronts a belief in a disease process the knowing will always triumph. Let's take a minute to examine the difference between a belief and a knowing. I will use a situation of swimming and we can examine what gives us a greater sense of empowerment, the belief or the knowing. I can certainly have a belief that I can swim simply based on the facts. I've seen others do it and I understand the concept of swimming lessons. Having this belief that I can swim is great, but since I haven't had the experience of swimming there will be an element of doubt. This element of doubt is tied to the emotion of fear of drowning and creates roadblocks to that which I wish to achieve. Remember in the case of a multiple personality, the person had no doubt that they were Steve or Sue. A knowing on the other hand comes from having had the experience of swimming that perhaps was taught when I was 3 years old. Now even 30 years later without swimming for 27 years, because I've had the experience, the element of doubt is removed and my belief has become a knowing.

I was never taught how to swim so I have a fear of water. So what you're saying is that since I haven't had the experience of swimming, I act on my doubt?

BLISS: Precisely, you and everyone else without experience. The emotion creates feelings that manifest into your reality. Use any scenario that you like which could be riding a bike or jumping rope.

The knowing eliminates fear and doubt and that makes all the difference in empowerment. So now let's apply this knowing to the world of addiction. When the belief of recovering fully from addiction becomes a knowing, it removes all doubt; the knowing will triumph. Our beliefs come with an element of doubt, because our beliefs originated from someone else, whereas knowing comes from within our own experience. Now we recognize that doubt is a powerful thought because it's tied to an emotion or to our feelings. Most doubtful thoughts are attached to the emotion of fear or uncertainty. So if thought is one of the most powerful forms of energy, we must understand that thought tied to an emotion or feelings determine what manifest into our reality. Words do not teach; you must have the life experience or experiences that give meaning to the words you hear and speak. To make any change whether it's an addiction or anything else, you must change a belief to a knowing.

So how can we do that?

BLISS: There's a simple process. It begins with a desire for change. This desire gives birth to new thoughts. This new thought attached to a willingness to step into a new experience holds the key to turning a belief into a knowing. From this knowing all the change you desire will then come into your reality. In truth it has no choice like a dam opening up to a river, the water must flow downstream. The awareness of your thoughts and the emotions attached to them are where all your present power exists. All of your power is in the present moment. Yet we spend so much time reviewing our past or looking into the future. The only importance of our past is to confirm whether our beliefs are true. Change your thoughts and change your perception of yourself.

This doesn't make sense to me because the 12 step program claims that we are powerless over our addiction. You seem to be implying that we're not powerless over our addiction, but in fact we have all the power?

BLISS: Let us lighten up a little bit everybody. This is not rocket science. This isn't so deep, its right in front of you on a conscious level waiting to unfold. The fact is if you don't have the power, who does? Once again we create our reality.

I would say our higher power yields the only power.

BLISS: So, your belief is that your purpose is to sit around aimlessly waiting to be infused with this power?

Not exactly but just the things that we don't have power over such as our addiction.

BLISS: This will be another shift in consciousness for some of you. It's kind of like Dorothy in *The Wizard of Oz*, when in the end she's told that she's always had the power within her to return home. That might be a little far back for some of you so how about a more recent example. Do most of you remember *Star Wars* and *The Empire Strikes Back?*

(Most agree.)

BLISS: Good. Remember the character called Yoda?

(Most agree.)

BLISS: Let me cut to the chase. There is truly only one step as Yoda so eloquently described to Luke Skywalker as he tries to move his ship with his mind from a swamp of mud. Luke said to Yoda as the ship fails to fully emerge from the swamp upon his trying, "I've tried and it doesn't work." Yoda simply responds, "There is no try; there is only do or do not." Those words ring a powerful truth. This refers to the ultimate truth of choice. As Luke gives up trying and turns away he notices that his teacher moves the ship from its place submerged in the mud and places it next to him on solid ground. Now of course, Luke's immediate response is "I don't believe it," to which then Yoda responds "And that is why you fail." Luke in that moment has a shift on a conscious level as he sees a creature much smaller than himself perform a task that he could not imagine himself doing with such ease. In Dan Millman's book, *The Peaceful Warrior* he relates the story of a wise teacher who has a student sit alone in a field, not to return until he has something meaningful to say. After a long period of time and many wrong answers, he finally finds the right answer which is "there are no ordinary moments." Now let this sit with you, in every one of those moments you have a choice. Yoda was right that the power you seek from outside of you is within you and has been there all the time.

You make everything seem so easy. Where is the gotcha?
BLISS: You make everything seem so hard. Easy does it. You know I've seen those 3 simple words "easy does it" on so many walls of programs that I have visited and yet for many it's still seems so hard. Choice is the ultimate power that we wheel around unconsciously. We think that shit happens and that we have no control over it. In truth, nothing happens to us that we do not bring into our experience. It's not by chance. Quantum physics teaches us that every action has a reaction. You are responsible for everything that shows up in your experience. So, you ask me if you are powerless over your addictions? Nothing can be further from the truth.

Sounds like you aren't really big on support groups?
BLISS: This will be hard for some of you to hear. Support groups are not conducive to self-empowerment. Support groups are there for people who need support. I believe you will not find many self-empowered people in support groups. And honestly we are talking about being self-empowered.

There are many people who successfully completed the 12 step program and have achieved sobriety for more than 20 years, so what do you say to that?

BLISS: I'd say that goes without question. Once again you must make the distinction between being in recovery and being recovered. Words have great power and the difference between those two words is enormous. Make no mistake I am not here to tell you that being in recovery is wrong for anyone. On the contrary, it's great for those that find lasting success there. I'm here to let you know that you have a choice. Somewhere someone has put a label on you that placed you in a group that's not worthy of bliss. Somehow you have held this label to be true. In truth you get to decide what label you want for you whether it's good or bad in recovery or recovered. Let me sum up the difference. Fear and bliss cannot coexist. Many people have 30 years of what they may call sobriety which is truly beautiful and maybe even fulfilling. Most also hold onto the deep rooted fear that they may one day return to their addictive behavior or drug use. To live in bliss is much like the bird that flies without the fear that its once broken wing may fail again. Consequently, if the bird is to fear the wing failing again, the bird will never truly experience the true joy of flying. When the bird soars across the sky, it knows it has recovered and has no fear of its past circumstance.

> ❝ Fear and Bliss cannot Coexist ❞

Either way, isn't it still flying?

BLISS: Perhaps, but at the core of its belief is fear and that emotion will steal its bliss. Just like flying across country on a Boeing 747, you can enjoy the flight with the feeling of tranquility or you could fear that there is a terrorist on board wishing to crash the plane.

So we are just supposed to simply change our beliefs and see things differently? And what do you mean about so-called sobriety?

BLISS: I hear the term clean and sober and sobriety thrown about all the time. Truthfully, cigarettes are filled with drugs. Coffee, tea, prescription drugs, soda and food are also loaded with all kinds of chemicals. In that case, very few on this planet could claim to be clean and sober.

> ❝ Change your thoughts and change your perception of yourself. ❞

Faith versus Fear

BLISS: Let's dive into the heart and soul of our beliefs, shall we?

Please do, I am sure that this is where the big gotcha comes in right?

BLISS: Yes this is the big secret so listen up. Everything is based on one question that has been asked by many great teachers in many different ways throughout history. I will paraphrase it for you. Now ask yourself this question. Do you live in a world of goodness and beauty or do you live in a world of evil, fear and scarcity?

Well there's war, terrorism, home invasions and drive by shootings so I'd say the second choice; scary. Now I suppose you're going to tell us that it's a wonderful world?

BLISS: It's not really that important how I view the world, but it's extremely important how you see it. Your answer to that question gives you an accurate look at your core belief system, which everything you experience comes from. So yes, if your core belief is that this is a dangerous world what you will see in your life experiences will come from that dangerous viewpoint. So if your answer to the question is based on watching the six o'clock news, you interpret experiences based on fear and will thus have fear based experiences. Stress and depression are at an all-time high, which correlates with the high sales of stress and anti-depressant drugs advertised during the commercial breaks of our news reports. On the other hand, if your core belief is that you live in a love-filled and beautiful world, you will tend to see more of that show up in your experiences. Remember that your perceptions create your reality.

So are you are talking about the two forces of the universe, good versus evil?

BLISS: Yes to some degree, but the point really is the understanding of the core beliefs you hold on to that determine your experiences. Reality is that there is only one force in the universe and you can flow with it or against it. The choice is yours. If it is your belief that there are two opposite forces that govern our world, that conflict will influence your experiences. The actual effect of the core belief may show up as a very subtle decision that you are not even aware of. Truthfully, our mind controls only 5% consciously, yet 95% is dominated by the subconscious. So we believe that we are controlled by our conscious mind when in truth we act upon our subconscious. To put it in terms as it relates to addiction for example, most people start by putting their attention on things that they don't want or miss.

You often hear people say "I hate using this drug. It's destroying my life." So what shows up in their experience is hating using the drug. Another example in everyday life is people that tell you they never have enough money. What shows up constantly in their experience is not having enough money. Most people activate in their experience what they don't want and then look for evidence of what they don't want showing up. You could actually put your attention to just the opposite for things that you do want and then look for evidence of it showing up. It's that core belief that there is a dark side of what you truly want and you activate it through feeling that dark side. So your experiences are activated by the emotion of something to fear such as lack of or not wanting. Consciously you would say why would I activate the things that I don't want. It is because subconsciously fear is the stronger emotion than the tranquility that your conscious mind strives for.

You have got to admit that there's evil and disaster on the planet. I mean just look around. You can't miss it.

BLISS: I'm sure there is, yet there is so much more good going on than evil or disaster. It's a simple equation. You have two dogs — one in the front yard that scratches and bites you and one in the backyard that's full of play and love. In which part of the yard do you spend your time? Your experience is determined by that choice.

So you're saying that if we say we are satisfied with what we have or don't use terms like "I hate," things would be different?

BLISS: As scary and simplistic as that may seem yes, but only when your true feelings and emotions are connected to your thoughts. Understand that the universe just gives you what you put out. It doesn't make judgments on what you put out. The universe doesn't know the difference between good and bad. It is just pure energy moving in the direction you choose. We can go with the flow of the universe or against it. As I stand across from Peter, there is a space or energy that we cannot see between us. The energy isn't good or bad it's just pure energy. What we both choose to do with that energy as it connects with our energy field is our choice according to our perception. So Pete may take the energy and decide to just go with the flow and continue to look for more of what he would love to show up in his experience. I might take that same energy in that moment and decide that I will fight against the things that I don't want in my life and constantly be on guard against them showing up. The universe is like a rapidly flowing stream and you have the choice to place your hand in the stream and let the water flow gently through. Or, you can also choose to put your hand in the rapidly flowing stream and push against it and attempt to capture and control the water in your hand.

Are you talking about God when you say universe?

BLISS: I'm talking about whatever you wish to call it. Even science has come to the understanding that the space between you and me is not empty. There is an energy field eminating from each of us. The bigger question is are you conscious of that and what it is doing? Most people aren't conscious and believe in luck, chance, and consequences.

Of course, because that's reality isn't it?

BLISS: You make your reality from your beliefs. We hear so many people talk about luck, when in truth as I said before, everything is energy. We are all a part of this energy field or one with the universe / God. We are not only the creator of our reality, but we create our energy vibration through our emotion and thoughts. I'll share this true story and see if you notice the unconscious shift between two thoughts of energy vibration switching in midstream. Back when I was in school learning to become a drug and alcohol counselor, we had a wonderful lady come speak to the class. Our teacher wasn't really big on hearing people's stories, yet for this occasion she honored the speaker's choice. She began by telling us how her life had spun out of control to the point where she lost her children, home, car, and freedom all in one day. Because of bad choices she had made in the world of drugs, the law had taken everything from her. After her time had been served, she began a battle to get her kids back into her life. Apparently her three children had been put in some type of foster care program. Now because of her past crime, she was told not only by the prosecutor but by her own attorney that she needed to sign papers forfeiting any chance of seeing her kids with the exception of Christmas until they were old enough to choose to see her. She told us how empty she felt and how the guilt and shame of her past became ever so present. In that moment she fought back the tears of anguish that she felt and said, "Somewhere in me I just had faith in my higher power and refused to sign the paper, my faith has always been strong." Her attorney reiterated how if she went up against a jury of her peers and lost, which she most likely would, she would most likely never see her kids again. The case did go to the jury and they decided in her favor to return her children to her. She paused for a second and then told the class, "but I was one of the lucky ones." I couldn't understand where her innermost beliefs and faith turned her into being one of the lucky ones.

So you're saying that luck had nothing to do with it?
BLISS: What I'm saying is that it's amazing how fast we turn over our power to someone else or call it luck. It is as if we are not worthy to believe in our own vibration and guidance.

I need to jump back for moment, Bliss; I'm still stuck on this multiple personality thing. Can you give us another example?
BLISS: What part of that are you stuck on?

That a person can just change their physiology by their change in belief. How does that happen?
BLISS: Actually the question is intertwined with the question on reality. Haven't you all heard stories of little old ladies lifting a car from someone to save their life, when we'd normally say that's not possible.

Yes, but isn't that adrenaline?
BLISS: Yes, we know that adrenaline is fired off from the body's natural pharmacy, but the action itself breaks all of the rules of what we believe to be physically impossible. Let's take adrenaline out of the equation and go back to the time when it was believed that it was humanly impossible for man to run a mile in under four minutes. Roger Bannister in 1954 broke that record by 2 seconds with a time of 3 minutes and 58 seconds. This was a record that had stood for 102

years. Less than 8 weeks later that record was broken again by another runner. This was not adrenaline rushing through the bodies of these 2 runners. It was their belief that they could run a couple of seconds faster than the previous record. Once Roger Bannister had broken through a collective belief that it was humanly impossible to run a mile under a 4 minutes, it took less than 2 months for this feat to occur again. The most astonishing example without question would be the placebo effect.

That's the study where they give you a water pill instead of medicine right?

BLISS: Yes, just recently they used five hundred people needing knee surgery in a study. Half of the group received the surgery and in the other half they made a cut as if they had done the surgery, but did nothing. One year later they followed up to find that there was no major difference in the two groups and all had improved. The only notable difference was that the non-surgery group reported fewer side effects. Many studies have been conducted where they gave the patient what they thought was a cancer drug to get rid of the cancer, yet in reality they were given only a water pill. Because the patient believed that they received a cancer drug, many developed bleeding gums and loss of hair. So, you can see once again the power of belief has a direct correlation to the physical effects on the body. Placebos are a common study used in research in many medical institutions. So let's address the question of reality. Are these people not creating reality from their belief in the effects of a pill? Here's a great one; how many times have you heard somebody say things always happen in threes? The real question is do they look for three things and then start a new list?

Yes, but it often occurs when someone I know dies, two more will soon follow, it happens all the time.

BLISS: So, if that's the way it happens, you must have a lot of nervous friends. In truth, people are transitioning all the time. How you number them becomes your reality. Your reality is what you have decided it is and you could just as easily say people always die in fours and that would become true as well. Somewhere along the way we have heard that things happen in threes and you look for evidence of it in your experience. Most certainly as that third person dies it becomes your reality, one you might even pass on to your kids. If your children look up to you with faith that you wouldn't say something that's not true, they'll adopt the same reality. Nothing malicious was done here just as nothing malicious is being done once someone tells you once an addict always an addict. They're just simply passing on their belief which is a thought they hold to be true.

So you don't believe that some of us have an addictive personality?

BLISS: No more addictive personality than any child has when he sees a toy that he wants on TV in June. I mean correct me if I am wrong guys, they wanted it yesterday not for Christmas. Your ego will never let you rest because it never wants you to become conscious. People get a brand new car and in less than one year they're eyeballing a hot new car that they wish to have next. We develop labels and phrases to separate ourselves such as "people like us," and "we have to take one day at a time." This shouldn't be a news flash. Everybody takes one day at a time. Oprah and Bill Gates only get one day at a time. Yet those who label themselves addicts act as if they are damaged goods and are in a special group that can only handle one day at a time. Imagine if we all had to handle seven days at a time. The diagnosis of being bipolar could become an epidemic.

Yes, but that's what they say in the program, we must always be aware because if we're not we could use again, isn't that true? I know several people who after being clean for 20 years have relapsed.

BLISS: Yes, I'm sure there are some who have but there are so many more who haven't relapsed. Again, people who label themselves addicts will look for that person who failed or relapsed to quantify their experience. You also need to realize that you are speaking of a group consciousness that believes as a whole that you could relapse. Group consciousness can be powerful or damaging depending on what is said. Let me give you a powerful example of group consciousness. Many people hold the belief that a relapse can happen at any time during one's recovery. It's relatively obvious and is backed up by statistics. Then you have a doctor who shares this belief and goes on national TV representing a celebrity. Now, in their statement to help justify this person's actions, they declare that relapse is a part of recovery. Every person who holds a label of an addict can now be relieved that they have relapses in them and they can breathe a sigh of relief. This is a group consciousness, a block of thought that is held to be true and now becomes our belief system. Similarly, we had a shift in consciousness about Swiss watches. At one time it was believed that the Swiss held the market on making watches. This was a collective or group consciousness because we all held it to be true. When someone came along and introduced the idea of using quartz instead of the existing windup method, the Swiss said; "don't tell us how to make watches." However, it's very rare to find a windup watch today. By the way, who are they that you speak of when you say they?

They, represents the experts in the field. Are you saying that they are wrong? I heard that once your brain shows damage because of drugs, it will last for the rest of your life. Also relapse comes from the damage to the brain that always wants that drug and is now being denied it.

BLISS: I am saying that they are giving you what they know from their knowledge and their beliefs. What you need to be aware of is your awareness. Doctors are good. We need them. Their contributions to our world are astronomical. Just as important is your own knowledge of yourself. Become conscious of the words you use such as "should have," "could have," "but what if," and of course the all important "I can't." These are all illusions that will keep you disempowered. That invisible energy that exists everywhere creates everything and you must come to the awareness that you are a part of what it's doing. Your brain will have a strong impulse to return to the substance that you are using and of course if you introduce the drug to your system the consequences will be immense. Still you play the biggest role in this process.

You just say that like it's so simple.

BLISS: Not only can I, I did. Learning how to think differently is the ultimate key to what you are seeking and yet the struggle is right there.

Let's take a little break and try a short exercise. I don't want all of you to go deep into your heads because this information must be learned through the heart and not through the head. You must not only hear what I'm saying, but you must feel it to comprehend it. So lets sit comfortably with our eyes closed in what is called a contemplative meditation. I will share a thought with you that I want you to let resonate through your soul. I don't know what your beliefs are but for those who believe in Jesus Christ try this, and for those who don't just bear with me for a couple of minutes. Even if you don't believe in Jesus, just take this moment and honor yourself for being. Gently close your eyes. Think about this thought that I'm going to share and let it flow from your spiritual chakra at the crown of your head down past your wisdom chakra or your third eye. Let it slowly continue down until it reaches your heart and hold the thought there. Okay ready here it goes; picture the word can't in your mind. Now see the word spelled out. Then imagine the last letter of the word as a cross. Okay, see the cross in your mind? Now contemplate this. **"Jesus died on the cross of can'(☦) so that we can."** Keep your eyes closed and let that flow down and into your heart without judging. Be still and gently become one with your breath. (Pause) Return to consciousness slowly and let it be.

In the Old Testament, the book of Exodus is the story of Moses, it is one of our oldest texts known to man. It takes place 1,300 years before the birth of Jesus Christ, that's 800 years before Lao Tzu, it is the only place that God's name is given by God. "And God says 'I Am That I Am'. Then in The Book of Joel 3:10, God says "Let the weak say 'I am strong.'" Why would you ever say in the world of addiction that "I Am An Addict"?

BLISS: For those of you who want a more scientific answer of the word *can't*, we can look in the dictionary. We know the word *can't* comes from the word *cannot* which by definition means the negative form of *can*. This is one the most overused words that we've carried from our childhood and still use unconsciously in our adulthood. The word *can* defined in the dictionary means having the ability and/or knowledge to do something. From the Heritage 2nd College Edition the meaning of the past tense *could*, means physical or mental ability. Also, it is defined as possession of a specified power right or privilege. Here again we can see the powerful difference in the words and their meanings. Really get this. I repeat that words have power and even more powerful is the meaning that you give to the words. You may be thinking that's not scientific enough as an answer, okay, so understand this; Dr. Masaru Emoto has done extensive study on the power of words and what they imply, which you can read about in his many books. Through the study of water, Dr. Emoto has shown how powerful words can be and the effects it may have on our physical bodies. From a method of freezing and crystallizing water, we can easily see the visual effects words play. By simply writing the word *love* on the jar before crystallization the effect afterwards shows the formation of a beautiful crystal, much like you would see if you were to look at a magnified snowflake. Whereas when the word is changed to *hate* on another jar and then crystallized the crystal that it forms is distorted. As words are changed, this phenomena continues consistently time and time again. Perhaps I will bring you some photographs of his work tomorrow.

So how does this affect our bodies?
BLISS: Our bodies are made up of 80 percent water.

Okay, so why have we always been told that we can't heal and we should never forget where we came from Mr. B?
BLISS: That's a great question, my one word answer would be "fear." Why are we being told in our news media that a lion escaped from a zoo in California and killed a man when we live 3,000 miles away? Is it so that we can look out for a loose lion in Vermont? Is there a new epidemic of lion attacks across the nation? Why is our media filled with warnings of things that could happen to you if you don't follow some advice? Maybe it's that we should all live in constant fear of "what if," and it could happen to you. Fear is played everywhere to get a response or to sell something. Fear is best defined as False Evidence Appearing Real. What I am saying to you is that if you choose to live in the world of fear, things you fear will continually show up in your experience. Today, there is talk of all kinds of strains of viruses. In truth, we are more likely to contract only fear.

Yes but there are bad things happening all the time, you can't ignore that, Bliss.

BLISS: No, I don't ignore it, I simply put my attention on what I want to encompass in my experience. The truth is, for every bad thing that happens in this world, a thousand good things occur at the same instant. Somehow those thousand things don't sell papers or wind up on the 6:00 news.

Remembering your past and where you came from is what makes us who we are today. Are you saying that's not true?

BLISS: You must remember your past is an old adage used to keep us in what I call recycling doom. If we really go back to where we come from, addiction would not be an issue, but let's not go back that far. You must relinquish your past for what it is: your past. Very similar to a snail it leaves a trail behind it as it moves across the ground yet is not a trail. If you were to examine the trail, it will tell you where the snail has been, but can't tell you the current status of the snail. However, if you were in the desert and came across a rattlesnake skin, you would certainly be concerned about where that snake is now. Your concern of where the snake was in the past or where it came from isn't quite as important as where it is now.

Esther and Jerry Hicks use the teachings of Abraham to show us a great analogy from our past. Abraham, the teacher, refers to the navigation system in your car. Abraham reminds us that you can program your navigation system to direct you from New York City to any street in San Francisco, California. The navigation system never asks you where you have been. The only information it needs is where you are now and where you want to go.

That being said, you can simply understand that if you wish to reach your destination, you must follow your guidance system and not stare into the rearview mirror. We know that it is a fact that if we get into our car right now and drive down the road staring into our rearview mirror, we are going to crash. It seems like a silly little simple example, but the realization of the crash is inevitable. So it is in life; if we spend all of our time looking into the past, we will crash, or as it is said in most programs, you will relapse. Caroline Myss, Ph.D. in her book *Why People Don't Heal* states the number one reason for this is because we bond to the wounds of our past.

So it's not important how bad our past is; but only where we are going?

BLISS: Honestly, most people aren't even accurate when speaking about the past. Most so-called addicts get so caught up with their addiction that the past gets distorted. Your past is your journey that brought you here to this present moment and the judgment of it being good or bad usually brings bad vibration to your now. Once again relinquish the need to judge.

Distorted? What do you mean?

BLISS: How old are you now?

GARY: Forty-two-years-old

BLISS: And what is the longest time that you have been clean and sober?

GARY: Almost 7 months about two years ago.

BLISS: How long have you been using?

GARY: Since I was 15.

BLISS: So would it be safe to say in all honesty that your longest period of sobriety was at least 14 years?

GARY: Technically, I suppose so.

BLISS: It's not being technical that is a reality but somehow we have created an illusion that says sobriety starts after the addiction. We must be very aware of the rules that we set up in our own minds that create our reality.

So you're saying that we should just forget about our past and move on, but my question is, what about all the people that know what we have done and who we have hurt? Are we supposed to forget about all that?

BLISS: If you are reading a book or watching a movie are you more concerned with how the book begins or how the book or movie ends? What happens to the characters in the middle of the story compared to how they turn out is often vastly different. You see, if you are the writer of your story, you get to decide what's going to happen in the next chapter. The characters in your story will react to who they become rather than who they were.

You don't think that we need to make amends to all those that we have hurt in our lives?

BLISS: Honestly, making amends is all about you not them. In truth you can say you're sorry all you want, but it doesn't change what has happened. What you become and the deeds that you do from now into your future is all that really matters. This doesn't mean that we can't repair relationships that we have damaged. What I'm saying is that they are best repaired through our present deeds and future actions. The difference is coming from a place of empowerment and not guilt and shame. We are used to telling our story from a place of guilt and shame. But they are the two lowest forms of energy. Dr. David R. Hawkins wrote a book based on a twenty-nine year study called *Power Versus Force*. In this study, he measures thought energy. On the top of the scale at a vibration of about one thousand, we have enlightenment. At the other end of the scale at twenty and thirty we find guilt and shame. From this understanding it would be insurmountable to raise anybody up the scale while vibrating at the energy level of twenty or thirty on a scale that measures to one thousand. You can't heal or help anybody when you're vibrating from the low energy of guilt and shame. Going around revisiting past situations hoping to improve them from a vibration of guilt and shame is inefficient.

> **FEAR** is best defined as
> False
> Evidence
> Appearing
> Real

Pilots and Bikers

Okay now you're talking about vibrations of energy that we vibrate at on a scale, of what?

BLISS: Precisely, we are energy and energy is always vibrating. You must raise yourself up from a low energy field to a high enough vibration that you can begin to heal. Moving up the vibrational scale is simply an awareness of how you feel and what you think. As you move yourself up the vibrational scale, you eventually get into a zone in which everything falls into alignment with what it is that you desire. You've heard athletes claim that they are in the zone and just can't miss. They either see the basketball hoop as very large or a baseball rotating so slowly that they can see the stitches. Michael Jordan said that when in the zone he could see a play unfold before it happens. What are they all talking about? They are talking about mental and physical vibration becoming one. Beginning with clear thought and stillness, everything radiates in a perfect flow of energy and alignment.

You are talking about great athletes not addicts like us!

BLISS: How fast you grab on to that label and hand away your power without giving it any thought. Yes, I am talking about athletes, many who were addicts at one time. Let's take an example and ask the big question. I'm sure many of you know the story of Lance Armstrong. Yes? Let's have a closer look. Before Lance Armstrong won the Tour de France he was stricken with cancer. This cancer was in his brain, his stomach, and his testicles. The tumor in his brain alone was said to be the size of a grapefruit. Lance was told not only would he never ride a bike again, but also his chance of survival was about 40% at best. In truth, after Lance beat the cancer, his doctor confessed that Lance's actual chances of survival were about 3% at best. As we all know, he beat this cancer and won the Tour de France seven times after remission. He went on to write a book describing this ordeal called *It's Not About The Bike*.

Once again you are talking about a great athlete that overcomes tragedy; how does that relate to us?

BLISS: That leads me right into the big question. In Lance's own words he describes the sport of cycling as a sport of denial. As he puts it, you must deny the pain that your body is in and overcome it with your mind. Does that sound familiar to anybody here? The most telling part of Lance's story in this battle with cancer was his mind. He would be the first to say that he isn't anyone special. But he did give credit to the power of his beliefs. He believed in his doctors, he believed in the treatment, he believed that he would ride again and most of all, he believed in himself.

Another key element for Lance was that he surrounded himself with people who believed that he would succeed. You see Lance Armstrong refused to listen to just the diagnosis; he put his focus on beating all odds.

Cycling is a sport of endurance and overcoming pain. So yes, in some ways cancer came up against a tough customer. Much like Michael Jordan being told that he wasn't good enough to make his freshman high school basketball team, Lance was determined. Statistically, children have a much greater chance of surviving cancer than adults. Lance Armstrong accredits that to the fact that children haven't learned all the lessons of failure that we adopt in our lives. In the end, he's not sure how much his own belief had to do with his survival. Lance believes that you have two choices. Give up or give it everything that you have. So the big question becomes what is the difference between these athletes and you?

CINDY: They have a God-given ability.

BLISS: So let's say there is a God that is unconditional love. Why would God give some people this ability and not others? Before you answer that question understand that the ability that they possess is in their mind first before it manifests physically. You see, if these two athletes just listened to the naysayers, they would have failed.

So you are saying I could win the Tour de France if I just decided to?

BLISS: I don't doubt anything about you because I have no idea of what's inside of your mind and heart. There were sponsors of Lance Armstrong who visited him on what they determined was his deathbed. Having a financial commitment, they tried and succeeded in a way to renegotiate their position. They too had no idea of what was inside this person's mind and heart. Once again I remind you, these sponsors pulled out prior to the Tour de France.

Examine others who've been told that something is impossible. Certainly someone told the Wright brothers that it is impossible to fly. Anyone who travels for a living is certainly glad that they didn't listen. Any good doctor will tell you first and foremost he has no idea what your mental capability of healing is because it can't be measured, just like they can't measure how much pain you actually feel. When someone heals himself from cancer or some other incurable disease without traditional medicine, it's often referred to as a miracle or that it had been misdiagnosed.

So how does this relate to my addiction?

BLISS: With all that we've talked about today let's re-examine the power we give to words such as addiction. And more importantly the deep emotional meaning we attach to the words. You've given all your power to the label, my addiction, as if you own it.

Pilots and Bikers

So all these people who label themselves addicts and go to meetings are wrong?

BLISS: Once again this isn't about right or wrong because in truth there is no right or wrong, just choice. Let me use this metaphor to bring some clarity to all this. I call it pilots and bikers. If you wish to accomplish anything in your life, get in alignment with what it is that you want. Here is what I mean; if you wish to learn how to fly a plane you cannot learn it by hanging around bikers. There is absolutely nothing wrong with hanging around with bikers except for the fact that they don't know how to fly planes. If it is your goal to know how to fly a plane, hang around with pilots.

That's obvious Bliss, but I'm not sure that I see your point. Are you saying that we should not be going to meetings and if so where should we be going?

BLISS: If you spend all of your time talking about motorcycles for a whole year, you'll know a lot about biking. Unfortunately, if your intention originally was to learn how to fly a plane, you are out of alignment. After a year of talking about motorcycles, you'll have no idea of how to fly a plane. What you spend your time talking about day in and day out will manifest itself into your experience. Therefore, if you spend all of your time in discussion about addiction and relapse, you will get more addiction and relapse into your experience. Naturally, if I spend all of my time learning how to fly a plane from pilots, chances are learning how to fly a plane will be in my experience. Remember in the Lance Armstrong story how he surrounded himself with doctors and friends who believed in the outcome that he wanted.

So am I wasting my time going to meetings because I feel that it helps to keep me sober?

BLISS: It's not really about good or bad. It's about what you want in your life. If what you want is to struggle every day with your addiction, then the daily conversation about that will be your experience. Get clear on what you really want. Do you wish to fly planes or ride bikes? Do you wish to struggle with your addiction or live in a feeling of bliss? It's really about what you wish to keep active in your vibration. If your daily discussion is on relapse, drugs, or just getting through the next day, these subjects will become your experience. You see it has to be that way because it is active in your vibration.

But there are people who have been clean and sober for 30 years. Are they wrong?

BLISS: Really try to release this right or wrong attitude; it comes down to what is right for you. If you ask your sponsor who has been clean for twenty-eight years if there is still a fear of relapse, the answer I assure you at the heart of the matter is yes. Because, at the essence of that question, there is fear and doubt attached to emotion. On the other hand, people who do not walk that path don't have fear or doubt. As a matter of fact, you will very rarely hear them speak about addiction and their past at all. So, the choice is yours: Which model do you wish to follow; peace and bliss, or fear and doubt? Very much like doctors, sponsors are loving and caring people, but that doesn't mean they know anything about living without fear of relapse. They're not right or wrong. That is just their sincere belief. The question that you need to ask is what is in their active vibration?

This is a pretty strong assertion Mr. B. I am not sure that I can go along with this because without the program I wouldn't be maintaining today.

BLISS: I understand and as I said, the choice is yours. The truth is if you changed your personal program, you wouldn't be here in this program. Now ask yourselves this: Would you like to maintain today or live in bliss? Which word makes you feel better "maintaining or bliss." It's important to note what you feel is more important than what you think.

So what you're really saying is that support groups aren't good.

BLISS: What you are feeling is the need to defend your belief rather then allowing a new possibility or concept to gently flow through your consciousness. Support groups are for people who need support.

Yes, but I don't want to relapse into drugs so I need to be aware of the possibility every day.

BLISS: What you resist will persist. We have had a war against drugs since the Reagan administration. It's not a surprise that what we are against still exists. By saying that you don't want something, you activate it into your experience. If your daily statement is "I hate being overweight," the universe will grant you what you say. So in response to your hating being overweight the universe will say okay you're a person who hates being overweight. Once again what you resist persists. Be clear on what you say and feel.

> " What you Resist will Persist. "

So then what should I say?

BLISS: First things first, and really get this; do not beat yourself up. You don't need a home run right away. Just get to first base. So if you are overweight, you do not declare, I'm so happy to be thin on day one. You just want to move up the emotional scale of feeling better about yourself. Therefore, you would say something like, I feel good today, or I am eating a little healthier today and taking good care of myself. In the case of your addiction, you could say I'm so grateful that I'm a little better today than I was yesterday.

This sort of sounds like fake it till you make it. Is this true?

BLISS: No, it is claiming that I am! You don't have to believe it one hundred percent in that moment; you just claim I am. You're claiming this not for your conscious mind that's filled with doubt, you're claiming it for all the new cells and their membranes as they become activated in your body.

ILLUSION

I'm sorry Bliss, I hear what you're saying, but you must also state the facts. The most successful movement to date is the one started by Bill W. There have been so many people helped by his movement.

BLISS: I agree wholeheartedly. You also must state the facts that this movement as you call it is 75 years old, but we have learned and evolved in so many ways. This is to say that there are easier ways to heal addiction; you don't need to be so hard on yourself. As I've said before, there are two ways to learn, through pain or insight; both are equally effective. I am not saying that it's old and outdated because there have been many great teachers on our planet even 500 years before Jesus Christ walked the earth. We have evolved in so many ways plus the insinuations of past lessons have also evolved.

The membership of AA is enormous so you can't be in denial of its success.

BLISS: I guess that's the point. I can be in denial of what is deemed success. Do I deem success never being healed? I like to choose my own destiny. You can follow the twelve steps of AA if you want; it's up to you. But remember, I said earlier, rejoice if you have the choice. You can choose to take a long guilt ride up the emotional scale knowing that you can never heal. I must go back to the point that you're talking about being in recovery, not being recovered. If your daily thoughts and talk is surrounded by fear, guilt, and shame, healing from the inside out cannot exist. I understand why people claim that they're friends of Bill; there is a feeling of being connected. There are many great thinkers who have come before and left great teachings. What now stands before us is the opportunity for each individual to think rather than being thought. If you truly want to get to the truth very few people really take the time to think for themselves. Most individuals react to what they see and believe that they are thinking. Each one of you has a guidance system within you that you mostly don't

ILLUSION

trust so you let the beliefs of others become yours. It doesn't really matter whether these beliefs are even true or not. This is the great illusion that we create. We tend to follow the herd rather than walk on our own. Simply put, if you follow the herd, you're going to step into a lot of shit!

I will relate this story to you about a 66-year-old client who had been on the downside of a two-year program and was looking at a release date in two months. He told the group of his success being clean and sober while in this program. Then he related his fear of being released and in his words he said, "Sure it was easy staying clean and sober in the program, but what happens when I'm out in the real world? I know that's the time it will get me." As those powerful words left his lips, we could feel the fear in his soul. I cleared a space in the room leading from the circle to the doorway. Then I asked him to look as I put a block between the circle and the doorway. I asked him to look at the space between the circle and the doorway and notice the block. While he looked at it, I walked over and removed the block and said, "This is an illusion that you have planted in your future and as easy as I removed it, you can also." The look in his eyes was of astonishment that this was something he was creating on his own. All the attention to what he doesn't want became a physical stumbling block in the midst of a clear path. Within the same week I had two clients tell me that things are really great, but they're still waiting for the other shoe to drop. Once again this is an illusion built on past experience. There are no shoes that drop; only those you create with your thoughts. Imagine being on a sober cruise on a bright and sunny day and someone brings a bottle of water in a gallon vodka bottle. What do you think everyone would do?

It's obvious that we would freak out because why would someone bring a trigger on the cruise?
BLISS: The trigger that you speak of is an illusion since the bottle is filled with water. Therefore when I speak of the difference of being in recovery, and being recovered, you can feel the difference in the emotions that are stirred up by this scenario. Once recovered, it would not matter what was in the bottle and triggers become illusions that you create with your mind.

I'm not sure I follow because certain things do trigger us; I don't see how that's an illusion.
BLISS: The meaning you attach to the trigger becomes your reality. You can change what the meaning is which changes the feeling and the emotions simply by choice. You can easily change the trigger of this vodka bottle into a realization that it is just a bottle. What substance is in the bottle has little or no bearing over my choice to drink the substance or not.

My sponsor has been clean and sober for 30 years and swears that he's just one drink away from returning to alcoholism. So is he creating his own reality?
BLISS: The world that he has created for himself is his reality. He also has the choice to believe that drinking was something he did in his past and now is not a vibrational match for his lifestyle. It's like in the Book of Job (*what I feared has happened*). The 30 years of sobriety is not a big telling mark; it's the belief system that holds him prisoner to his fear or illusion. Changing your belief system transcends time. He can be living a successful and happy life living his current belief. He has the choice to live a successful and happy life without the fear of returning to past behavior by simply changing his belief system. Fear keeps us in the box, and others warning us not to step outside of the box is the great illusion.

PHARMACEUTICALS

BLISS: We are trained to give all of our power away and just react. We don't think; it just becomes social conditioning.

You have this innate power to tap into your own body's pharmacy and heal yourself. The belief today is that there is a pill for everything. Don't get me wrong. Pills have their place, but they should not be controlling every emotion and feeling that we encounter. We are allowing pills to shut down our body's natural pharmacy. Please, by a show of hands, is there anyone here not on some pharmaceutical drug currently? (No hands go up.)

Now let's review our guidance system that we keep altering with illegal and legal drugs. Thoughts create feelings. Change your thought pattern and you can change your feelings. Feeling creates emotions that drive our reality. You can have all the positive thoughts and feelings that you want, but if your emotion is based on fear, you will manifest that fear into reality.

I have a strong regimen of pills that I take and quite frankly it gets damn confusing. You think I should just stop all my pills?

BLISS: Knowledge is power; know thyself. I would never say to just stop taking all of your pills. I am not a doctor who can give you medical advice. Take some responsibility for what you put into your body. Discuss with your doctor what you really need and what you don't need. Each person is different. Understand yourself. If you were going to eat a completely healthy raw diet, some things will work well for you and others will not. Finding your pill regimen confusing is very understandable. Just imagine what it's like for an alcoholic to be on a pill management regimen. Most severe alcoholics aren't aware of what day it is. How can they be expected to manage their medications? Honestly most medications for those we label addicted are just traded as currency to get what the addict really wants.

Pharmaceuticals

Be aware that we live in a society that pushes pills, not much different than your corner drug dealer. A lot of it is just for profit, not necessarily anything that you really need. Do your own study; watch how many commercials are selling pharmaceuticals, disguised as something that you might need. Drugs with long names meant to give the feeling of pleasure and relief. Then we are given an array of symptoms so that we can pick one out that fits our situation. Finally, printed as small as possible or said extremely fast are the side effects. We are even prescribed drugs for depression that aren't proven to have any effect on depression, yet are accompanied by many side effects. Oh by the way, death is often listed as a possible side effect. If you've ever been told that there are no side effects, you're probably not being told the truth. We live in the biggest pill popping society in the world. It's amazing because at one time food was used as medicine.

The best pharmacy is the human body. There are many contaminants in our food that can damage our natural pharmacy. The drugs that we take to treat incurable diseases are mind-boggling. Think of all the money that has been spent in research alone and yet there are no cures. Ask yourself why. The truth is it's not cost-effective to cure disease. You've been told how many times that you'll have this disease for the rest of your life. You've been led to believe a lie. I will go so far as to say that one of the leading causes of death in our world today is conventional medicine. Although many deaths are called heart attack or stroke, the actual cause in many cases is the use of medications. Today's conventional medical practice in many cases is literally malpractice because it does not deal with the cause of the illness. I know these are bold statements, but many medical and nutritional experts agree.

But you said yourself that you are not a doctor so how can you make such statements?

BLISS: A great question with a simple answer. I just make that statement, based on the many documented cases and verified healings that I've witnessed. These so-called miracles don't really get a lot of press. We live in the information age; look up the information. Before you put a blocker in your brain or take one pill for depression and another for anxiety, become informed. Just because you've seen it on a forty-two inch flat screen television, doesn't make it true. The biggest disease that we have on the planet is fear sold daily on the flat screen and radio. Early prevention is touted as one of the best ways to ward off disease. You may even go to your doctor and he'll tell you "You're fine, but come back in six months and we'll see if we can find anything then." You may get a report that says this is high or this is low. In fairness, doctors are trained to find things that are wrong, more so than trained in studying wellness. We are often given sincere medical advice from our doctors, but in many cases, although the advice is sincere, it may also be wrong.

I don't know Bliss; you're walking a slippery slope. I'd have to trust my doctor when it comes to my body, don't you think?

BLISS: I agree. I would trust the most educated doctors, not just any doctor. There are two schools of thought. Let me give you an example. There are doctors who believe that the best treatment for cancer is radiation and chemotherapy. There's another camp that believes a change in diet and a strict protocol could create a high pH and change the alkalinity of the body to eliminate cancer cells in the body. The difference here is that one camp knows that radiation and chemotherapy kills all cells in the body and hopes the cancer cells die before you do. The other camp knows that you can kill cancer cells while other cells will restore you to health. I ask you, which camp would you trust your body to?

Yes but we know that if cancer is caught early, radiation and chemo can work.

BLISS: Yes, and we also know that it damages your immune system. We also know that diet and raising your pH also works and is less invasive. Once again were talking about knowing thyself. Drugs have not taken away your ability to learn. Do your own research and be aware of who is funding what you read. If you're on the web, go past the first 5-10 highly funded websites or research articles. You'll find much more truth deeper and further away from the money. I know this sounds controversial, but we are searching for truth. How important is this? It's your body and life that we are talking about.

You're asking us to believe you. How can we know with certainty that what you're saying is true?

BLISS: You can listen to someone who successfully walked away from addiction or you can hold on to your current beliefs. You're fear of change is keeping you holding on to an old belief system. Some of you will continue your current path and some will take heed and expand your reality. The proof is always in the pudding. Your expansions of truth will be individual. Though I think you will find that the easiest way to have success is to find someone who has succeeded and follow what that person has done. As I said earlier, I'm not only a man named Bliss, I live a life of bliss. If you're not living that type of life, change what you are doing.

You make it sound so simple, but it can't be that simple.

BLISS: The struggle you are having is with your perception, not whether it's simple or not. Here is a simple truth: Many medications cause damage to different organs in your body. Therefore when someone dies of a heart attack, they actually die from the side effects caused by the pharmaceuticals used over a period of time. Of course, we are told that a heart attack was the cause of death. This is simply not true. However, the end result may constitute a heart attack. Most medications address the symptoms but not the cause.

> "The best pharmacy is the human body."

MEDITATION

BLISS: As I promised in the beginning, we would come full circle and end with meditation, *which ties everything neatly together*. You have heard me say time and time again: Know thyself. This is where meditation comes in. We spend so much of our lives looking for answers in the outside world, when the true authentic gifts begin within. When you get quiet and start to meditate, you connect with the divine and the true essence of yourself.

Oh man, I have tried to shut down my mind and meditate; it's just not happening.

BLISS: I hear that all the time and it always makes me laugh. I too started from that same place of "I tried and it didn't work." Actually, when you first try to meditate and quiet your mind, you may find screaming monkeys racing through your head. Your thoughts run rampant, and you find out how crazy your mind has become. If this has been your experience, you're quite normal, not incapable of meditating. The mere thought, "I can't meditate" is a trick of your ego. The ego never wants you to find a spirit. It's a big "I can't process rather than I can." Let's first get rid of some of the misconceptions about meditation. First of all, your brain is a receptor; its job is to think so you should never stop it from having thoughts. Second, you don't have to be sitting on the floor like a monk not moving for hours. Third, anyone can learn to meditate. It is a practice not a perfection. If you've had the experience of joining a gym you'll find it quite difficult in the beginning. A lot of people quit and others adapt by making their workout a habit or routine. Meditation is very similar. Some people find it a hard discipline while others see it as creating a blissful state in life. They change the meaning from discipline to something blissful. If you are a person who is very hyper or energetic, running or walking might be meditation for you. For others, Yoga or Chanting might be a meditative practice. I personally have no desire to scale the mountain to reach the top, but I can appreciate the serenity

MEDITATION

that must be found in that practice. There are many different forms of meditation, but the key to each one is probably the word focus. Learning to focus from within is a key component to meditation. As your focus becomes more accurate in time, you might find a sitting meditation quite appealing. Meditation is a calming of the mind and spirit so that one can reconnect with the silent energy force that flows through each of us. Call it God, source, or universal flow; it doesn't matter what you call it. When you get quiet and begin to feel from the heart and allow yourself not to be distracted with the thinking mind, all possibilities come together. The limitations that we put on our lives become possibilities in reality. Illusions begin to dissipate and our greatest fear begins to reveal itself. That fear is the fear of our highest potential that is one with source.

I'm not sure that I believe in all that or even more important that I could ever reach that place in myself. But you say it's possible for everybody even if he doesn't believe in God. I also have understood that our greatest fear is death.

BLISS: The answer is yes and yes. We are all part of this great universe on some level, regardless of what we choose to call it. When you learn to meditate, you break all boundaries from your separateness with all that is. We have fought many wars and lost many lives in the name of what to call it. Meditation will bring you to a place where everything just is. I heard this once. You can call it God or if you're dyslexic call it Dog, the meaning through intention is the same. When you begin to reach your highest potential and connect with the source that is everything, the fear of death dissipates as the illusion is revealed. We are so much more than what we believe ourselves to be. Meditation reconnects us with a part of ourselves that we most often ignore.

How do you go about learning to meditate?

BLISS: There are so many different techniques and ways to meditate and eventually you'll find which one best fits you. But to start, become the witness of your life. Start to realize that there is a part of you that has been present since the day you were born. Start to notice that this witness has been with you through your early childhood, your teens and most importantly is with you now. That witness that has been present throughout your life doesn't age. Our body without any doubt shows and feels age. Yet the witness that has watched this progression doesn't have a body; it just resides in one. We often believe that who we are is 95% physical when perhaps in truth it is 5% physical and 95% non-physical. The witness is that part of the 95% non-physical consciousness that resides in everything. It has been said: "We are not human beings having a spiritual experience; we are spiritual beings having a human experience." When you begin to know, not believe, but know that statement is true, your view of the world will shift forever. This may seem as if it has nothing to do with meditation, but it's a perfect starting point as you begin to look within. This awareness of your relevance on the planet and in the universe illuminates the importance of now. We begin to realize that life is a series of moments in which we live. When we begin to capture those moments in the now, the universe will become our teacher. This is important because there are universal laws that govern life on this planet such as the Law of Attraction. It says that what you most focus your attention on will show up in your life. The Law of Attraction does work, but another equal law: *If you focus a great deal on things you do not want, they too will show up.* And the law that supersedes the Law of Attraction is: *What you want is on its way, but it will take time.* However if what you don't want is attached to stronger emotions than to what you do want, what you don't want will show up almost immediately.

Meditation

Now to answer your question. To meditate, simply began to get quiet and notice each thought without judgment. Allow thoughts to pass through your consciousness without attachment. Without attachment means to releasing any emotion attached to the thought. There are many techniques to meditation, but the important thing is to just begin.

Eknath Easwaran, a great teacher of meditation, was in a colleague's library. The gentleman asked his teacher, "Have you read this book on meditation?" The teacher answered, "No I have not." Repeated questions about different meditation books continued with the same response. Finally the colleague asked, "How do you know so much about the meditation? You haven't read any of these great books on the subject." In response the teacher said, "I meditate. I don't have time to read all of these books on how to meditate."

Yes, but how do I quiet my mind? Whenever I try, so many other thoughts interfere.

BLISS: Allow yourself to watch each thought travel across your consciousness like a cloud pattern traveling across the sky. Release your judgment about what the cloud might look like or be. Simply notice the cloud and when it moves past your glance, go back into the blue sky until the next cloud comes into your vision. Returning to the blue sky is the same as noticing your breath which you are often instructed to do while meditating. As you become more skilled in this practice, you may return to focusing on the beat of your heart. Another way of looking at this is to imagine walking on the sidewalk with a little child. There will be times when the child walks off the sidewalk to look at a flower, a rock or a butterfly. You pause without judgment and eventually continue on the sidewalk to your destination once again returning to your breath or the path. The less attachment you have to each of your thoughts, the deeper you will be able to meditate. Your brain will eventually tire of you not paying attention to each thought and begin to create larger periods of silence. As we begin to honor those periods of silence and honor the practice of meditation, self-awareness is heightened and our purpose for being becomes apparent. This very gentle process leads to a connection of spirituality with all things. On this conscious level we truly begin to know ourselves.

> **❝ Reality is not limited to the perception that we have traditionally used. ❞**
>
> *- Paul Stamets*

Epilogue

Ask yourself this question. What is the opposite of love? The answer is actually Fear. I have emphasized these two points of love and fear all through this book. *God is love, and has given YOU all that you already need.* I paraphrase what Jesus said, *All that I can do, you can do, and even greater things.* Stop and ask yourself what that means.

> " God is love, and has given you all that you already need. "

> "Follow your bliss and the universe will open doors where there were only walls."
>
> - Joseph Campbell

About the Author

Larry Daniel Webb founded Insight Alternative Addiction Healing (IAAH) in 1996. Previously, Larry lived a life of addiction and homelessness. During that time he was told by his oldest sister that he had ruined his life and would never be able to recover from his addiction. That simple statement did not resonate as truth with Larry, and if it was true how could that be? How can someone just look at another person and determine their future? From that day forward, Larry went on a mission to discover the truth. Without meetings, a program, or medication, Larry walked away from the world of addiction and embarked on a journey of self-discovery. He went from homelessness to managing a 6 million-dollar business and living a life of bliss. This book will take you through his journey and what he discovered to resurrect his life.

Acknowledgments

George Hayes Jr., LCSW, LADC

Dr. Donna Marks

Rev. Winn Henderson, M.D.

Lauren Doninger, EdD, LADC, LPC

Angels in my Corner

Joy Bershtein

Cathy Winn

Jayne Power

Carolyn Geida

Robert Geida

Books That Are A Must Read

Freedom From Addiction 3
by Rev. Winn Henderson, M.D.

Exit The Maze:
One Addiction, One Cause, One Cure
by Dr. Donna Marks

The Meaning of Bliss
Bliss is a magnified emotional state of joy, personal fulfillment and happiness without need of outside influences.

The Meaning of the Butterfly
The butterfly represents spiritual rebirth, transformation, creativity, endless potential, vibrant joy, change, ascension, and an ability to experience the wonder of life.

Made in the USA
Middletown, DE
12 December 2020